CHESAPEAKE BAY COOK BOOK

Bayfood Edition

BY

FERDINAND C. LATROBE, II
The Diamond Back Terrapin, etc.

Illustrated by *Yardley*

WILDSIDE PRESS

FOREWORD

These receipts, or recipes (have it as you wish), have been tested by palates—not by science.

Many of them have proved their efficacy, and their deliciousness to the detriment of the author's and the illustrator's *embonpoint*. Others they have seen cherished by relatives, and still others have been enjoyed by guests. So be it the author, the illustrator, the cousin or the acquaintance—the concoctions have all pleased some gourmand.

They have been gathered from far and wide. Where most of them originated we do not know. They came to us in recollection, in manuscript, in clippings, in ancient household treasures, and in research, with Mr. Richard Armstrong, into the Chesapeake Bay's history of the past four centuries.

Therefore, we thank the dead and the living for their contributions towards what we hope will be another worthwhile ennoblement of that glorious natural heritage—The Chesapeake Bay, so proudly and rightfully boasted of by Maryland and Virginia.

The Chesapeake's Seafood, or, more appropriately, Bayfood, falls into three categories—THE SHELLFISH: the Oyster, Manninose, Clam and, still-a-few Scallop; THE CRUSTACEANS: the Crab and Crawfish; THE FIN-FISH: about 200 species, of which the most notable are the Croaker or Hardhead, Rock, Shad, Herring, Perches, Spanish Mackerel, Blue Fish, Squeteague, Sea Trout, Norfolk Spot, Mullet, Butterfish, Flounder and Eel. Each and every one of these edible Fishes reaches such a perfection of flavor in the waters of the Chesapeake that it is nigh onto impossible to say which is the finest; and, such is their appreciation by those who live upon the Bay, that, in describing each individual of the tribe, the dictionary's adjectives will be pretty well used up.

As to the importance of Fish in our diet, Savarin observed, no nations were so courageous, "As those that eat Fish. Fish contains a large quantity of phosphorus and hydrogen, the two most combustible things in nature . . . it is therefore, a most heating diet, and I have been led to think that the genesiac sense is moved by eating it. [Especially, because of] the different manners of preparing Fish, containing all the seasonings that are irritating, and the various juices the Fish imbibes being highly inflammable and oxygenise in digestion. . . . Fish, though less nutritious than flesh, and more succulent than vegetables, is a *mezzo termine* which suits all temperaments, and which persons recovering from illness may safely eat." When one realizes the wonderful health enjoyed by the Chesapeake's inhabitants, and recollects that, since the Indian wars prior to 1776, the soldiers from the tidewater have led the van of all of our armies, Savarin's observations upon the courage and the vitality emanating from a Fish diet are well proven.

Apropos of the selection of Fish for the table, Savarin also pertinently wrote,—"The nose plays the part of the sentinel, and always cries 'Who goes there.' All sapid bodies are necessarily odorous, and therefore belong well to the empire of one as of the other senses." Thus, your nose, your eye and your touch should guide you in the purchase of Fish, that you may not discover too late "unpalatable food is not wholesome." To determine the freshness of a Fish, make sure it is thick and firm, with bright scales and stiff fins, the gills a very likely red, and the eyes full and prominent. While it will have a "fishy" odor, it should smell "sweet," or "all right."

The average housewife receives her Fish cleaned, and ready to put in the pan. But, should a present *au naturel* be received, the cleaning of a Fish is neither a messy nor a tedious job. First, hold the Fish by the tail, and, (for want

4

of a proper instrument), scrape the scales off, toward the head, with the back of a knife. Then, insert the point of the knife into the vent, (not too far, if it be a roe Fish), and rip the belly open. The intestines may then be easily removed, and the gills taken out, either by cutting them loose, or by beheading the Fish. Rinse and wipe the Fish thoroughly, to remove all of the blood, particularly that adhering to the backbone.

Then, wipe it dry, and put it into the refrigerator until you wish to use it. If that be not for a day or so, put it in the freezing compartment. When thawed out quickly, none of the flavor will have been lost.

If you wish fillets, skin the Fish as soon after being caught as is possible by removing the fins along the back, and cutting off a narrow strip of skin along the back-bone. Then, loosen the skin at the gills and pull it off toward the tail. Allow the knife to follow the skin, to help separate it from the flesh.

The Fish has been a religious symbol ever since the earliest days of Christianity, ranking with the ship, anchor, Good Shepherd and the palm, at the end of an epitaph. It is a complete formula in itself, significant of a confession of faith.

As in the Greek word for "fish"—ιχθυs—each letter stands for an aspect of the Redeemer.

ι ιησουs.....Jesus
χ χριστοs...Christ
θ θεου.....of God
υ υιοs.....Son
s σωτηρ....Saviour.

"Jesus Christ, the Son of God, the Saviour."

The institution of eating Fish on Fridays is lost in antiquity. But the serving of Fish before meat dates back to Queen Elizabeth, when in 1562-3, there was enacted, for the "Maintenance of the Navie," to encourage fishing and thereby provide sailors for the fleet, an order requiring Fish to be eaten alone three days a week. However, as in our laws today, there were many strange quirks. One provision allowed the purchase of an exemption for Wednesdays and Saturdays, for 2 shillings payable to the poor box. A second provision permitted, on Wednesdays, a meat dish to be served with every three dishes of Fish. Therefore, those who could not afford the exemption put three dishes of Fish and one of meat upon the table for Wednesday's dinner. And, to show their lack of intention to abuse the law—the Fish was served before the meat. Such has become both the custom and the fashion today.

We must warn the reader that the secret of Chesapeake Bay cookery is, first, its primitive simplicity. When we eat Oysters, Crabs, Canvasback or Terrapin we wish their peculiar piquancy alone to delight our souls, untarnished by the strange flavor of some garnish. Second, as few palates agree upon the strength of seasonings, their quantity has been left to the cook's imagination, as of old—and pitiful is the cook who is devoid of that essential agreeability.

FERDINAND C. LATROBE, II

6

TURTLES AND TERRAPIN

The lower Chesapeake Bay is a common resort for the oceanic Green Turtle, who wends his way northward, from the tropical waters, to turn into the Bay. He is a tid-bit for the tidewater Virginians, as well as the traditional repast of the Lord Mayor of London.

Scattered throughout the tidewater country is the Snapping Turtle, which infests the streams and creeks of the Chesapeake's tributaries. He makes a delicious dish; and, when the Diamondback Terrapin was worth its weight in gold, the Snapper was the poor man's luxury.

The nobleman of the tribe is the famous Diamondback Terrapin,—the luscious, but barbaric dish, which even today is the appreciation of the ultra-ultra circle that does not have to read Emily Post. We have read of the feasts of Lucullus, of the Sybaritical suppers of the iron and steel barons,—yea, of even those of the butter and egg men,—but only amongst the financial and social hierarchy does one hear of the unobtrusive Terrapin Suppers that have launched more deals and "kicked-up" more social climbers, than all of the notorious Saturnalias.

Though the Diamondback Terrapin lacks the spontaneous exhilaration of Champagne, it, together with its notable companions, the Chesapeake's Oyster, Clam, Crab, and Duck, supposedly contain those aphrodisiacal qualities so

7

essential to Savarin's sixth sense—the genesiac sense. This imagination might be construed as a fact, when we note the large families amongst the town and ducking club members; or count the bachelor quarters that are tossed over the orphan asylum walls.

★ GREEN TURTLE SOUP

Hang the Turtle by its back-fins, cut off its head, and let bleed until the next day. Then, separate the shells, being careful not to break the gall bladder; remove that bitter object, with the entrails. Cut up the breast meat; cut off the fins near the shell; take out the green fat, and put each aside. Break the shells, and boil until you can remove the gelatinous substance. Save the water, and in it stew the head, fins, liver, heart and meat, with 1 pound Ham, 1 dozen Cloves, 2-3 Bay Leaves, 1 Onion, adding some Savory, Marjoram, Basil, Thyme and Parsley. When tender, strain all except the herbs into another pot. These, with the Onion, go into another pan, with ¼ pound Butter, 2-3 heaping teaspoons Sugar and 1 quart of Madeira, to simmer slowly, until needed.

Melt ½ pound Butter, thicken with Flour, add 1 pint of the water the shells boiled in, and boil 1-2 minutes.

Now, into a large container, strain the Herb, Onion and Butter mixture; Green Fat; Gelatinous substance, from the shells; meat, cut in small pieces, and add yolks 12 hard boiled Eggs, made in balls, (see recipe p. 9), juice 2-3 Lemons and dessert-spoon of Red Pepper. Cook until it steams, and then serve.

If the soup be put in a stone crock, covered and kept cool, it will keep for some time, and improve with age. To use it when old, heat but do not boil, and add more wine.

★ SNAPPING TURTLE

If you wish, you can try the traditional manner of fattening your Turtle by putting it in the hog's slop barrel.

Clean by scalding in boiling water, until the skin on the legs can be rubbed off. As Turtles are generally very dirty, you will probably need to put through several waters. Re-

8

move the bottom shell, and take out the meat. Be careful not to break the gall bladder,—throw it away with the intestines. Wash shells thoroughly, and put into the upper shell the meat, liver and heart chopped in small pieces; add several slices of Bacon, Butter, Salt, Black Pepper and a few thin slices of Lemon, judging the proportions by the size of the "Bird." Put the bottom shell on, and run into the oven, in a pan with sufficient water to cover the Turtle. Stew for an hour or two; then pour in 2 cups Milk, and boil 10-15 minutes longer. Take out and serve with Sherry.

★ EGG BALLS

(To help out Turtle or Terrapin.)

Hard boil 8 Eggs in salted water, and then throw into ice water. Pound the yolks into a paste; moisten with yolks of 3 raw Eggs, and season with a couple of pinches of Salt, dash of Red Pepper, Nutmeg and Mace. If you are going to use them in Terrapin, see what the real eggs look like, then mold the paste into imitation ones and put into the Turtle, or Terrapin, about 2 minutes before you serve it.

★ DIAMONDBACK TERRAPIN

In 1893, the Maryland Club sent its celebrated corps of epicures to Philadelphia, in response to a challenge, to teach the latter city how to properly prepare Diamondback Terrapin. The dish prepared by the estimable "Uncle Frank" Hambleton, the leader of the invaders, was awarded the prize over the typical Philadelphia floured concoction done by Mr. Struthers, of the Rittenhouse Club's contingent.

The Indians, and later the Negroes, roasted their Terrapin in the coals of an open fire. When stoves came into vogue, the Terrapin was baked in an oven. But, here follows "Uncle Frank's" winning receipt for Terrapin prepared in the accepted manner of the last and present generations of Baltimore gourmets. You will notice it is almost *au naturel,* and is not contaminated with flour, cornstarch or milk. Incidentally, Terrapin is very easy to clean, and simple to prepare. It was considered an invigorating dish for invalids, and, as we have said before, from a social standpoint—a Terrapin Supper ranks supreme.

9

Terrapin 5 inches long have tender meat, but few, if any eggs. *Counts*, 7 inches long, are sufficiently tender, and generally have plenty of eggs. Therefore, it is wise to buy a half-a-dozen of each. (The male "Bird" is never eaten). Drop them into boiling water, and boil until the skin can be rubbed off of the claws. Then, take out, and when cool enough to handle, pull off the lower shell; take out the intestines, break off the feet, (save the legs), and throw away. Disjoint the legs, and rub the skin off. Carefully break open the liver, so as not to break the gall bladder, which looks like a green olive. If you do break it, instantly crumble away all of the liver that the juice touched, and wash the rest under a spigot as you run the risk of your dish being bitter from the gall. Clean the web from the eggs, saving every one, regardless of size. Pick all the meat out, and pull it into small pieces. (Some tidewater authorities like to re-boil the shells, and use the gelatinous substance from them).

Put into a double boiler, or a chafing dish, the broken-up liver, heart, meat, legs (with the bones), and eggs, add about ½ pound Butter, Salt and Black Pepper to taste. Let it cook until the Butter has formed a gravy, then add Sherry or Madeira to taste, and serve. If it is prepared in a chafing-dish, at the table, the individual adds his own Sherry.

A dozen Diamondback Terrapin will serve 6 ordinary persons, or 4 gourmands. Burgundy or Madeira should accompany the dish.

★

THE OYSTER

So, wrote the poet Gay—

> "That man has sure a palate cover'd o'er
> "With Brass or Steel, that on the rocky shore,
> "First broke the oozy Oyster's pearly coat,
> "And risked the living morsel down his throat."

From time immemorial, Chesapeake Bay Oysters have been famous the world over. Before the days of fast transportation, and of ice, they were pickled and sent even abroad. With the arrival of the railroad, Chesapeake Oysters began their nation-wide migrations, first to Frederick and Cumberland, later to St. Louis, and then to the Pacific coast, while every sailing of the trans-Atlantic steamers carried the Bay's Oysters to Great Britain and Europe. The first travelling Oysters were either in the shell, or steamed and canned. Later, it became possible to shuck them, pack them in ice, and ship them in a condition to render their use a simple one, by the housewife; and, at the same time retain the delicious flavor of a fresh Oyster.

The custom of eating Oysters only in the months having the letter R, dates back to medieval days, when Harrison wrote, in England, "Albeit our Oisters are generally forgone in the foure hot moneths of the yeare, that is to saie, Maie, June, Julie and August, which are void of the letter R." Jeaffreson remarked that they were neglected during those summer months, "not only for want of flavor and condition, but also because they were thought provocative in hot weather of the same immoralities as in France are attributed to excessive indulgence in Mackerel . . . It is strange how divers kinds of fish, albeit commended by the church as food fit for religious seasons, have been accused of stimulating vicious appetites and encouraging evil propensities."

Be that as it may, Oysters are one of the most healthful foods that we can eat. They contain both minerals and salts, especially iodine, besides many of the essential vitamins necessary to a nutritious diet.

The flavor of the Oyster varies according to the salinity of the waters in which it lives. As the Bay waters range from almost fresh water to that of ocean saltiness, the Oysters of the Lower Bay, generally served on the half-shell as raw Oysters, have a delicate salty tang in comparison with the brine of ocean Oysters.

★ RAW OYSTERS

Raw Oysters should be served very cold, but not near freezing point. If you have deliciously flavored Oysters, they need no more than a drop of Lemon juice to accentuate their flavor. If they be not quite salty enough, a tiny pinch of salt dropped along their gills a few minutes before serving will add the wished-for tang. To dip good Oysters into cocktail sauces completely destroys the flavor of the Oyster, and is a sinful waste. It is far better to eat the Oysters for themselves alone, if you like them, and enjoy the cocktail upon crackers.

★ COOKED OYSTERS

In cooking never boil Oysters, or Clams—it makes them as tough as wet leather. Simply keep the temperature below boiling point; and the gills of Oyster or Clam will curl, to indicate they are cooked. The liquor of shellfish should

12

always be boiled and skimmed to remove the dirt, which arises with the foam. As it burns very easily, keep it stirred.

★ ROAST OYSTERS

Either put the shell Oysters upon hot coals, upon a metal plate over a fire, or in the oven; and cover them with an old bag. When they are *thoroughly* roasted, (nothing being more insipid than a half-cooked Oyster), with the shells open, the Oysters curled, and a little brown, serve instantly. Place before each person a saucer of melted butter, mixed with Salt and Pepper, in which to dip the Oyster.

★ A LA SOUTHERN MARYLAND SOCIETY

Put a strip of Bacon upon each half-shell Oyster, run them in a very hot oven, and bake until the Bacon is browned and Oyster is curled. Put them upon a plate, pour melted Butter over them and serve hot.

★ PIGS IN BLANKETS

Drain large Oysters, and wrap each in a piece of Bacon; skewer with toothpicks. Then fry until they are curled.

You must stir them, so as to cook the Bacon all around.

This is a delightfully attractive dish for an afternoon, or buffet party.

★ PANNED OYSTERS

Allow 6-12 Oysters to a person. Drain, put in a cast iron skillet, with sufficient Butter to cover the bottom about ⅛ inch deep, and add Salt and Pepper. Let the Oysters cook slowly, constantly stirring, until their liquor and Butter form a gravy. Serve on toast; pour the gravy over them.

★ OYSTERS HAMPTON

24 large Oysters, 3 large chopped Mushrooms, 1 cup chopped cooked Chicken, Bacon, ½ cup Cream, yolks 2 Eggs, 1 tablespoon chopped parsley, ½ teaspoon Onion or Lemon juice, 1 tablespoon Butter, 2 tablespoons Flour, Salt and Pepper.

Bring Oysters to a boil, drain; boil and skim liquor. Take ½ a cupful of the liquor, add the Oysters chopped fine, and simmer until they are curled; about 10 minutes. Add Chicken, Cream, Mushrooms, Onion or Lemon juice, Parsley, Salt and Pepper, blended Butter and Flour, stirring constantly; add beaten Egg yolks, and when thickened, turn out to cool. Cut the mass into pieces, roll into small cylinders, wrap each in a slice of Bacon, skewer with a toothpick. Then dip into a French, or thin, fritter batter, and fry in boiling fat to a nice brown.

★ OYSTER CROQUETTES

These are made the same way, except the mass is rolled into croquette shapes, dipped in Egg yolk, then into Bread Crumbs, and fried to a nice brown. Serve with a Cream Sauce, flavored with Celery Salt.

★ OYSTER STUFFING
For Turkey or Chicken

To a Bread Crumb stuffing add as many drained Oysters as you wish, seasoning with Salt and Pepper, and moistening the stuffing with boiled and skimmed Oyster liquor.

★ OYSTER FRITTERS

Drain 1 pint of Oysters; boil and skim liquor. Chop the Oysters, (you need about 1 cupful), put back in half their liquor, and stew until the mixture thickens, seasoning with Salt and Pepper. Then strain them, and proceed as with Manninose Fritters. (see p. 21) Or, mix into any left over hot-cake batter. Oyster Fritters are very rich, and a few will go a long way.

★ BROILED OYSTERS

Drain the Oysters. Take 2 cups of liquor to every 2 dozen Oysters, (if they are large ones), boil and skim it. Put 1 tablespoon Butter in a cast iron skillet, brown, add 2 tablespoons Flour, and mix till smooth. Add liquor, bring to a boil. Season with Salt and Pepper, and keep hot. Now, broil the Oysters, then throw them in the sauce, and serve, preferably upon buttered Toast.

14

★ FRIED OYSTERS

Drain and dry the Oysters, season with a little Salt and Red Pepper. Handle them carefully, so as not to tear them. Beat an Egg with 1 tablespoon boiling Water, ½ teaspoon Salt. Then, if the Oysters are small, fit two together, dip in Bread Crumbs, then in the Egg, and repeat until you can pat them into a nice shape. Fry in deep fat, (hot enough to brown a crust of bread), to a golden brown. Lift them out, and drain on brown paper. Tomato ketchup and Cole Slaw are inseparable from Fried Oysters.

★ OYSTERS WICOMICO

Drain 1 pint Oysters. Beat an Egg, add 1 tablespoon boiling water, ½ teaspoon Celery Salt, or pounded Celery Seed. Dip the Oysters in Egg, then in Cracker Crumbs, repeating until thinly covered. Saute in about 4 tablespoons Butter. Serve, either with a Cream Sauce seasoned with Celery Salt, or with a gravy of their liquor added to the Butter, Salt and Pepper. Serve 2 Oysters upon a quarter slice of toast.

★ OYSTERS FRICASSEE

2 dozen Oysters, ½ pint Milk, yolks 2 Eggs, 1 tablespoon chopped Parsley, 1 tablespoon Butter, 1 tablespoon Flour, Salt and Pepper.

Drain Oysters; boil and skim liquor. Then stew Oysters in the liquor, until they curl. Melt the Butter, add Flour, mix until smooth, add Milk, and bring to a boil; add the Oysters, ½ cup of liquor, Salt and Black and Red Pepper. Stir till well heated, then add yolks of Eggs lightly beaten, and chopped Parsley. Mix thoroughly, and serve.

★ DEVILED OYSTERS

2 dozen Oysters, 1 cup Cream, ½ cup Cracker Crumbs, Butter, Salt and Pepper.

Drain and chop the Oysters. Put in a sauce pan with 1 teaspoon Butter, Cracker Crumbs, Salt, Black and Red Pepper and Cream, and simmer about 5 minutes, mixing thoroughly. Then, put into a baking dish, sprinkle with

15

Bread Crumbs, and bits of Butter; put in a moderate oven, and bake until a nice brown.

★ SCALLOPED OYSTERS

The amount of Oysters, etc., depends upon the size of the baking dish. Drain Oysters; boil and skim liquor. Then put in the dish alternate layers of Oysters and Bread Crumbs, sprinkling each layer with Salt and Pepper. Add, if you like, some crumbled cooked Bacon. Let the last layer be of Bread Crumbs and bits of Butter. Moisten the dish with half Milk and half Oyster Liquor; and bake about ½ hour in a hot oven, to a nice brown.

★ OYSTER SOUP

Drain 1 pint Oysters, boil and skim liquor; then boil liquor with 1 pint water, 1 cup Cream or Milk, 1 tablespoon Butter, Salt, Black and Red Pepper, Nutmeg, and finely chopped Celery, or Celery Seed. Thicken with Flour and mix thoroughly. 20 minutes before serving, add the Oysters, and let simmer until they curl.

★ OYSTER BROTH

(See recipe for Clam Broth, p. 22.)

★ STEWED OYSTERS, No. 1

1 pint Oysters, ½ wine glass Sherry, 1 tablespoon Vinegar, 1 heaping teaspoon Cracker Crumbs, Salt and Pepper, Nutmeg, Allspice.

Drain Oysters; boil and skim liquor. Then boil the liquor 5 minutes, with the other ingredients, excepting the Wine and Vinegar. Then, add the Oysters, and let simmer until curled; add Wine and Vinegar, and serve.

★ STEWED OYSTERS, No. 2

Drain 1 pint Oysters; boil and skim liquor, season with juice of 1 Lemon, Mace, Nutmeg, Salt and Pepper. Add Oysters, and let simmer until they curl.

★ OYSTER PIE

Soak 2 slices of Bread in 1 cup Milk, and mash them up. Add 2 beaten Eggs, 2 tablespoons Butter, Salt and Pepper, Nutmeg. Then add 1 quart Oysters, (with the liquor boiled and skimmed), fill the pie; put on a crust and bake to a nice brown.

★ OYSTER LOAF

Hollow-out a loaf of stale Bread, brush it with Butter, put in hot oven to brown. Then fill it with Creamed Oysters, and put it back to thoroughly heat.

★ CHESAPEAKE PIE

Line a deep dish with pie pastry. Put in a layer of Crab meat; season with Red Pepper, and grated Lemon Peel, mixed with mashed yolks of hard boiled Eggs, moistened with Butter. Then, a layer of drained Oysters, season with Salt and Pepper, Mace, Nutmeg. Top with Butter rubbed with Flour. Two more layers should be enough. Pour in 1 cup liquor, boiled and skimmed, and 1 cup of Cream or Milk. Put a crust on, pierce it, and bake in a moderate oven until a nice brown.

Anciently, this pie was decorated with balls encircling the crust, made of chopped Oysters, mixed with Bread Crumbs, grated Lemon peel, yolks of hard boiled Eggs, Mace, Nutmeg and fried in Butter. They are worth the trouble.

★ OYSTER SOUFFLE

2 dozen Oysters, 1 cup Milk, ½ cup Cream, 2 tablespoons Flour, 3 tablespoons Butter, 4 Eggs, Salt and Pepper, 1 tablespoon Sherry, 1 cup Bread Crumbs.

Melt Butter, stir in Flour, add Milk and Cream, Salt, Black and Red Pepper, and Bread Crumbs. Mix thoroughly, and let come to a boil, add Oysters, chopped fine; and simmer until Oysters are curled, about 10 minutes, then add Sherry. Take from fire, add beaten Egg yolks, stir till smooth, fold in beaten whites. Pour into a buttered dish, and put in moderate oven for about 15 minutes, or until a nice brown. Use a light hand.

★ OYSTERS ARMSTRONG

When you pan your Beefsteak, and turn it for the last time, fill the skillet with Oysters—to cook in the steak's juices. When you take the steak out, pour the Oysters over it. This is a real man's dish.

★ CELERIED OYSTERS

Saute 1 pint of Oysters, with 1 tablespoon chopped Celery, Salt and Pepper, in about 2 tablespoons Butter. As you take them from the fire, add 1 glass of Sherry. Serve on Toast.

★ OYSTERS FLEETWOOD

Drain 1 pint Oysters; boil and skim liquor, then put the Oysters back into it, and stew, with Salt and Pepper, Mace, Nutmeg, and a little Butter and Flour, to slightly thicken the liquor. Then remove the Oysters and chop fine. Cut the tops from a bunch of green Asparagus, and stew until tender in just sufficient Oyster liquor. Then put the Asparagus and the Oysters into the latter's cooked liquor, and simmer about 5 minutes, mixing thoroughly. Dip Toast in boiling Water, Butter and lay upon a hot dish, and pour the Oysters and Asparagus over it. Serve hot.

★ OYSTER CHOWDER

Line a dish with Bacon, put in a layer of sliced Potatoes, cover with Tomato ketchup, then a layer of Oysters, Salt and Pepper, and pieces of Butter, pour over Tomato ketchup, and so forth, until dish is filled. Lastly, pour in Oyster liquor, and stew about ½ hour in a moderate oven, until Potatoes are cooked.

★ OYSTERS AND BACON

1 pint Oysters, 3 slices Bacon, Salt and Pepper.

Drain Oysters; boil and skim liquor. Cut the Bacon into small pieces, and fry to a nice brown; add the Oysters and liquor, and cook until Oysters curl. Then remove the Oysters, and put in a hot dish. Let the liquor boil away a little, add Salt and Pepper, and pour over Oysters. Serve hot.

★ OYSTER ROLL

Roll biscuit dough thin, in small pieces, cover with Oysters and a little Butter. Roll up, and bake in a hot oven until a nice brown.

★ OYSTER GIBLETS

Either take left-over Chicken or Turkey Giblets, or saute fresh ones, put them upon a skewer, with strips of Bacon and large Oysters; and broil until the Oysters are curled.

Serve upon toast, with a sauce of Oyster liquor, Butter and Lemon juice.

★ OYSTERS ITALIENNE

1 pint Oysters, ½ cup ground Old Ham, 1 cup Tomatoes, ½ chopped Onion, 1 tablespoon Butter, 1 tablespoon Flour, ¼ pound Macaroni, Salt and Pepper. Parboil and blanch the Macaroni. Drain Oysters; boil and skim liquor. Melt Butter, stir in Flour, add Ham and Onion, and brown. Add Tomatoes, Macaroni, about 1½ cups Oyster liquor, and cook until fairly thick. Then add Oysters, Salt, Black and Red Pepper, and simmer until Oysters curl. Serve hot.

★ NEWBURG, OR CREAMED OYSTERS

(Also a sauce for either 3 dozen Oysters, 2 pounds Crabmeat, or Shrimp).

1 heaping tablespoon Butter, 1 tablespoon Flour, stir till smooth; add 1 cup Cream, and stir thoroughly, add 1 teaspoon Salt, Black and Red Pepper; add Nutmeg, and yolks of 2 Eggs. Then add Oysters, and stir until they are curled.

19

If you wish a Newburg—simply add 1-2 tablespoons Sherry; and when you make Newburg, you must not cheat, but use real Cream, and plenty of Butter.

Add cooked, chopped Mushrooms, and you have *Oysters a la Bechamel.*

THE MANNINOSE AND THE CLAM

The Chesapeake Bay is inhabited by two species of clams— the Manninose, (pronounced Man-no), often called in Virginia the "Butterfish", which is the long-snout soft shell clam identical with the famous Clam of New England; and the little-neck Clam, that the Northerners call the Quahog.

Manninose are widespread over the Bay's bottom, from the Atlantic Coast to the Chester River. In form, it presents two elongated soft or thin and brittle shells, enclosing a yellowish flesh, from one end of which protrudes a black snout capable of great extension. It lives buried in the sand, with snout stuck out into the water, to capture its food. When the tide goes down, the snout is withdrawn, and the blow hole remains in the sand, bubbling occasionally to tell of the animal below.

They are taken by digging them out; and, if you are not quick enough to get the fork, or spade, below them, and turn them out on the first attempt, you will be astounded how fast the creatures can wiggle down further into the sands; often faster than you can dig to catch them. The Manninose is the richest morsel produced by the Chesapeake Bay, (always excepting the Oyster Crab). It is reputed to contain many essential vitamins, particularly that conducive to good eyesight; and ranks first in the Bay's food which is said to have aphrodisiacal qualities.

The flavor of the Manninose and the Clam varies according to the salinity of the waters they inhabit. Those from the saltier waters are considered the most tasty. Like the Oyster, the Clam's liquor is, from both a nutritious and a delicate viewpoint, equal in value with its meat.

★ MANNINOSE SOUP

Put Manninose in a bucket of fresh water, to let them rid themselves of the sand in their snouts; or split the snouts, and wash the sand out.

Shuck them, chop fine, and boil a dozen or so in their own liquor. Then, skim, and strain through a fine sieve into a saucepan; thicken with Bread Crumbs, add a bit of Butter, Salt and Pepper. As boiling toughens shellfish, the meats should be thrown away, or ground very fine if you wish some in the soup.

★ MANNINOSE FRITTERS

Steam open a couple of dozen Manninose, (enough to make a cupful of minced meats). Put the latter in a saucepan, with about half the liquor; and stew for half-an-hour, until a little thick. Add a little Salt and Pepper, and strain.

Make a batter of 3 Eggs, 2 cups Milk, 1 cup Flour; mix thoroughly, and stir in the strained Manninose. Drop into boiling fat, from a spoon, and fry to a light brown. Drain, and serve hot.

★ FRIED MANNINOSE

Open the Manninose, split snouts, and wash out the sand. Drain a few minutes, then dip in a thin batter of Egg, Flour, Salt and Pepper, and fry in deep fat to a nice brown.

★ MANNINOSE CHOWDER

1 pint chopped Manninose, 2 cups chopped Onion, ¼ pound chopped Bacon, 1 quart water, less Manninose's Liquor.

Boil all, except Manninose, half an hour. Then add Manninose, 2 cups Potatoes (sliced, or cut in pieces), 1 tablespoon Sugar, 1 teaspoon Salt, ½ teaspoon Sweet Marjoram and Summer Savory, mixed, Black and Red Pepper; and simmer

21

until Potatoes are done. If you have some Sea Biscuits, break and soak 2-3 for 5 minutes in water, and add them 5 minutes before the dish is done.

★ CLAM BROTH

A simple and quick delicious seafood dish, equally adaptable to Oysters.

Shuck 1 dozen Clams, saving the liquor. Strain, boil and skim liquor. Then gradually add to liquor about 2 cups Milk, 1 tablespoon Butter, ½ teaspoon Salt, Black and Red Pepper; and ½ teaspoon Celery Seed, if you wish. If you want the broth thick, blend 1 tablespoon Four with the Butter. Chop, or mince the Clams, and add to the above; then let simmer until the Clams curl.

You may add a couple of Sea Biscuits, soaked, and broken, a few minutes before the dish is done. The whole process takes only 15-20 minutes.

★ STEAMED CLAMS

Wash and scrub Clams in the shell, in several cold waters. Put in a pot, allow 1 cup water to 2 dozen Clams. Preferably, have a grating to keep the clams above the water. Cover, and steam until the shells are open, and the meats almost separated from them. Then serve in the shells; wrap in a cloth to keep them warm. At each place have a saucer of melted Butter, Lemon or Onion Juice, Salt and Pepper, and Clam Liquor, to dip the Clams in. Serve the Liquor, hot, with Salt and Pepper, in cups.

★ DEVILED CLAMS

2 dozen Clams, 1 Onion, 1 Egg, ½ teaspoon Worcester Sauce, pinch dry Mustard, Salt, Black and Red Pepper, ½ teaspoon Vinegar, Bread Crumbs.

Drain Clams, and chop fine. Boil and skim Liquor; mix Clams, Onion chopped fine, beaten Egg, Vinegar, Salt and Peppers, Bread Crumbs, and moisten with the liquor to make a fairly stiff paste.

Then, either stuff in Sweet Peppers, or in Clam shells, sprinkle with Bread Crumbs, and bake about an hour in a moderate oven.

22

★ FRIED CLAMS IN BATTER, MARYLAND STYLE

Mix together yolks of 2 Eggs, 8 tablespoons of Flour, ¾ teaspoon of Baking Powder, ½ cup of Milk, and Salt. Fold in beaten Egg whites. Dip drained clams until lightly covered, then fry in deep hot fat.

★ FRIED CLAMS

Prepare the same as Fried Oysters. See p. 15 for recipe.

★ CLAM FRITTERS

Prepare the same as Manninose. See p. 21 for recipe.

★ CLAM CHOWDER
A La Casserole

If you wish this for Friday nights, you can leave out the Bacon.

Drain 2 dozen Clams; boil and skim liquor. Several slices of Bacon, 6 medium Potatoes, 2 cups Tomatoes, 1 Onion, any left-over Peas, String or Lima Beans, Carrots, Corn from the cob.

Chop Clams, and Bacon, dice Potatoes, slice Onion, and add sufficient of the other ingredients to fill a two quart Casserole. If you wish, add 2 or 3 Sea Biscuits. Stir the mixture, season with about 1 teaspoon Salt, Black and Red Pepper, ½ teaspoon dry Mustard, 1 teaspoon Celery Seed. Cover with Bread Crumbs, and pour in the Liquor. Cover, and bake in a moderate oven, 25-30 minutes, until Potatoes are tender; then, remove the cover, and brown.

This is a square meal.

★

SCALLOPS

Scallops are not specifically a Chesapeake Bay product, (though some do live in the lower Bay). Nevertheless, as they are caught along the Atlantic Ocean side of the Eastern Shore, we may consider them as a tidewater delicacy.

★ FRIED SCALLOPS

Cover with boiling water, let stand about 3 minutes, drain and dry. Dust with Salt and Pepper. Dip into beaten Egg, then into Bread Crumbs; and fry in deep boiling fat. Serve with Tartar Sauce.

★ STEWED SCALLOPS

1 pint Scallops, 1 pint Milk, 1 tablespoon Butter, 1 tablespoon Four, Salt and Pepper.

Wash Scallops in cold water, and drain. Let Milk come to a boil; add Butter rubbed with Flour, then add Scallops. Stir and cook about 5 minutes, season with Salt and Pepper, and serve. Add a little Sherry, if you wish.

★

THE CRAB

The Crab, as we know, was one of the notables in mythology. For the edification of those who prefer the crustacean upon the table, rather than upon the bathing beach, Lineo sent the Crab to bite the big toe of Hercules whilst fighting with Hydra of Lerva. In Chesapeake Bay country, the Crab has always been a foremost delicacy, comparable with the Oyster, Terrapin and Canvasback Duck. The soft-shell Crab is regarded as the *"Ne Plus Ultra* of the lovers of good eating." Godman told us that in 1819 the Bay's Soft Crab brought two dollars a dozen; and ten years later it was fried, placed in a tin butter kettle, covered with lard, and shipped to Philadelphia as a rare delicacy. Not too many years ago, one of Baltimore's familiar sights was the Crab man, usually a venerable colored man, dressed in a white apron, carrying a huge basket covered with a blue and white plaid oilcloth, slowly meandering down the streets, or haunting the railroad stations, crying his wares—"Deb'lled Crabs! Crabs! Deb'lled Crabs! Come git y're Deb'lled Crabs!"

★ SOFT CRABS

Since the Crab wears his skeleton on the outside, nature also so arranged that when he gets too fat for his bony confine, he sheds it for a larger one to hold him until he becomes stouter and again expands. Therefore, periodically the Crab is a "Peeler," just before he sheds, to become a "Soft Shell"; then, as the new shell stiffens, he is a "Paper shell", or "Buckram"; and then a "Hard shell." As one may imagine, in the Soft-shell stage, the Crab is at his fattest, (or synonymously, richest), period. His mere film of a shell is also edible, to make him a completely luscious morsel.

25

★ FRIED SOFT CRABS

When you buy Soft Crabs, be sure they are all "kicking"; then, turn back the pointed ends of the shell, and scrape out the "deadmen," or the fingerlike, membranous lungs; take off the "apron" from the back, and cut out the mouth and eyes. You do not remove the claws, or the "feelers," or legs. Dip the Crab in beaten Egg, then, lightly, into Bread Crumbs, mixed with a little Salt and Pepper, and fry 10 minutes in deep boiling fat. If they be "Spiders," or very small Crabs, they will be even more delicate if they are sauted in Butter. Serve hot, with Tartar Sauce, and quartered Lemon. Garnish with Parsley.

★ PICKLED SOFT CRABS

Clean and boil in salt water as many Crabs as you wish. Drain, cool, and place them in a crock. To sufficient Vinegar, to cover them, add Salt, Black and Red Pepper, Cloves, Allspice and Mace; scald, then pour over crabs. Let them cool; and serve the next day. A delicious dish.

★ THE OYSTER CRAB

The Soft Crab is often considered the Chesapeake Bay's greatest delicacy; but the richest, if not a more delicate, crustacean is the Oyster Crab. This little lady (because the male has never been found within an Oyster), is about ¼ inch long, sometimes all white, but more commonly striped with red, and round like a berry; and, while you cannot easily make out the perfection of her appendages, a tiny pinch upon your tongue will tell you that she has claws to nip with. The Oyster Crab is not a parasite, as it lives on tiny organic matter flowing into the Oyster's gills, which the Oyster cannot consume.

When eaten raw, "as they come" with Oysters on the half shell, it is considered a rare treat by the gourmand. When cooked in any quantity in an Oyster stew they add a magnificent flavor to the dish. But, when the Oyster Crab is Newburged, as a sauce—it is exquisite. And foolish is he who imagines he can eat any quantity of it. No Bayfood equals this minute morsel in richness, and we all know what happens from an over-indulgence of stimulating foods.

★ HARD CRABS OR CRABMEAT

In days gone-by, you had to catch your Crabs, steam them, and then pick them before you could enjoy the hundred and one unsurpassable dishes that Crabmeat can be turned into. Many years ago, the trick of canning Crabmeat was discovered; but the product could never equal the taste of fresh Crabmeat. Later, when refrigeration was developed, it became possible to pick the Crabs at the wharves at which they were landed, and ship the fresh delicious meat far and wide, with all of its flavor retained. So, today, the housewife can purchase an attractive package of fresh Crabmeat, ready to be incorporated into whatever receipt she wishes to follow.

Crabmeat is ordinarily put up in three packages. "Clawmeat" has a distinct "nutty" flavor, for which reason it should be part of every dish of Crab. Because it is slightly dark and a bit crumbly, the average housewife overlooks it—and thereby misses the enjoyment of its flavor. "Regular" is the white meat of the Crab, in large or small pieces, as it is picked. "Flake" or "Lump," the large, unbroken pieces of meat, make a most attractive dish—particularly a salad. (See also Newburg Sauce recipe, p. 19.)

★ STEAMED CRABS

This most primitive and wanton manner of eating Hard Crabs is a delightful one, provided you can take a bath immediately after the feast. If you are convenient to a Crab dealer who knows how to season the Crabs for a "Crab Feast," it is wise to benefit by his steaming equipment. If, however, you must cook them yourself, as many gourmands prefer to do, proceed in this manner, assuming you have a five gallon kettle, that will hold about 4 dozen Crabs. Put into it about 2½ inches of water, with ½ cup Vinegar, dessert-spoon Dry Mustard, dessertspoon Salt, dessertspoon Celery Seed, level teaspoon Black Pepper and ½ teaspoon Red Pepper. Dump the Crabs in, (seeing that everyone is alive), and boil for 25-30 minutes, when they will turn a brilliant pink-red; then turn out and cool. If you have a grating in the bottom of the kettle to keep them above the water, that they may only steam, they will be much nicer.

To serve, cover the table thickly with newspapers, dump the Crabs in the center—and go to it. First, pull off the feelers and claws; pry off the apron, and the back shell; remove the fingerlike deadmen, and the intestines (the yellow mass surrounding the latter is savory fat); get the meat out according to your own method, and break the claws, both first and second joints—so as to enjoy the piquant meat therein;—all the while being supplied with plenty of cold beer, and a dish cloth for a towel. Finally, roll the newspapers up, with the debris inside, put the mess in the garbage can; and if you have not timed your party with the collection of that cart, put the can as far from the house as possible; and, go take a bath.

To those who do not inhabit the Chesapeake Bay tidewater, a Crab party probably sounds horribly barbarous, but here it is accepted as exotic in the highest fashionable and epicurean circles. It equals the as-messy watermelon party so popular with the younger generation.

★ FRIED HARD CRABS

To get full flavor, remove back claws carefully from live Crabs, and clean them by removing aprons and deadmen—in the same manner as preparing Steamed Crabs to eat. Save the yellow-colored fat. Then, Salt, Pepper and Flour the Crabs and fry to a golden brown. Put the fat through a colander, add Pepper, Salt, Flour and a little water, thicken to gravy consistency, and place in the hollow of the Crabs when done. Serve hot.

★ CRAB GUMBO A LA MUNROE

Scald 6 Hard Crabs; throw away the feelers; break, or crack the claws. Clean the Crabs and break into 4 pieces. Throw them with the claws, into ½ gallon water, season highly with Salt, Black and Red Pepper, and Celery Seed, if you like it; and boil down about one-fifth. Fry 3 slices of Bacon, lightly, brown an Onion in the fat and add to boiled-down soup; with 1 pint Okra, cut in small pieces, ½ pint Lima Beans, 2-3 ears of uncooked Corn, cut from cob; throw the cobs in, but remove before serving. 1 little hot Red Pepper can be used instead of the Ground Pepper, if you wish. Simmer for several hours, until the vegetables are very tender, almost falling to pieces, and the Crabmeat is falling out of the shell. Taste and season as it cooks. This is a meal in itself.

★ CRAB SOUP A LA PENROSE

Scald 2 dozen Crabs; throw away the feelers, and crack the claws. Clean the Crabs, and break into four pieces. Boil a knuckle of Veal, until the meat falls from the bones. Then, remove the bones, mince the meat, put back in the broth, add 3 pints of Milk, the Crabs and the claws, 2 tablespoons Butter, 1 stalk finely chopped Celery, Salt, Black and Red Pepper, and Nutmeg to taste, and cook until the Celery is tender. Just before serving, add 1 wineglass of Sherry.

★ CREAMED CRAB SOUP

1 pound Crabmeat, 2 cups Milk, 1 cup Cream, 2 tablespoons Butter, 1½ tablespoons Flour, 2 hard boiled Eggs, Salt, Black and Red Pepper, Sherry to taste.

Melt Butter, stir in Flour, add Milk, Salt, Black and Red Pepper. When heated, add Crabmeat and Cream. Heat and mix thoroughly, add chopped Eggs, and Sherry to taste. Garnish with sprigs of Parsley. This is a very nice soup to serve in cups.

★ CRAB TANGIER

1 pound Crabmeat, 4 slices chopped Bacon, 1 cup chopped Celery, 3 cups cooked diced Potatoes, 1 small chopped Onion, 1 teaspoon chopped Parsley, 2 cups Milk, 1 quart water, 1 tablespoon Butter, 1 tablespoon Flour, 2 teaspoons Salt, ¼ teaspoon Black Pepper, dash Red Pepper, ¼ teaspoon Celery Seed, Paprica Pepper.

Fry Bacon, and Onion; add Celery and water, and boil 15

minutes. Add Potatoes, Salt and Pepper, Celery Seed, (if you like), and boil a moment before adding Crabmeat—to boil 15 minutes. Then add Milk, Butter rubbed with Flour, and thoroughly heat. Color with Paprica Pepper, and add Parsley. This is a Crab Chowder.

★ CRAB CLIO

Boil 1 large Eggplant and let cool; scald and skin 6 large Tomatoes and press water from them. Chop up cold Eggplant and Tomatoes, mix in 1 lb. Crabmeat, Salt and Pepper, add 1 tablespoon Butter, 3 beaten Eggs. Then, put in baking dish and cover with Bread Crumbs. Bake 30 minutes—or until nicely brown.

★ CRAB DORCHESTER

1 pound Crabmeat, 1 chopped Onion, 2 cups Tomatoes, 1 cup Consomme, 1 tablespoon chopped Parsley, 2 tablespoons Butter, 1½ tablespoons Flour, Salt and Pepper.

Saute Onion in Butter, do not brown, add Flour and stir until smooth. Add Tomatoes and Consomme; when well heated add Crabmeat, Salt, Black and Red Pepper, and, if you like, a pinch of Dry Mustard. Heat and mix thoroughly, and color with Paprica. Serve poured over toast, garnished with the chopped Parsley.

★ CRAB BISQUE

1 pound Crabmeat, ⅓ cup of Rice, 1½ pints Milk, 1 cup Cream, 3 tablespoons Butter, 2 cups water, Salt, Black and Red Pepper and Nutmeg.

Cook Rice to a mush, in the Milk, and mash through a fine sieve. Melt half the Butter, and add the Crabmeat. When well heated, add water, and mashed Rice and Milk. Boil about 10 minutes, then add rest of Butter, Cream, Salt, Black and Red Pepper, and Nutmeg. Mix thoroughly. Add ½ cup steamed Rice, and mix before serving.

★ SCALLOPED CRAB

1 pound Crabmeat, 1 cup Tomatoes, 1 cup Corn, cut off the cob, 1½ cups Bread Crumbs, ¼, or more, cup Milk, 3 tablespoons Butter, Salt, Black and Red Pepper.

Put a layer of Bread Crumbs in the baking dish, then one of Tomatoes and Corn, sprinkled with Salt and Pepper, and bits of Butter, then a layer of Crabmeat, similarly sprinkled, and so on until filled. Cover with Bread Crumbs, and moisten with Milk. Put in a hot oven, and bake 30 minutes to a nice brown.

★ DEVILED CRABS, No. 1

Melt 2 tablespoons Butter, stir in 1½ tablespoons Flour mixed with ¼ teaspoon Salt and a good pinch of Black Pepper. When smooth, add 1 cup Cream; bring to a boil for about 2 minutes, season with Red and Black Pepper, and a pinch of Mustard, according to how "hot" you wish the mixture; add a little Celery Seed. As it cools, add about 1½ pounds Crabmeat to make a stiff mixture. This must be done carefully, or you will mash the Crabmeat. Fill the shells, do not compact the mixture, mound high, sprinkle with Bread Crumbs; run in a hot oven, and bake until a nice brown.

★ DEVILED CRABS, No. 2

Melt 1 teaspoon Butter, add ½ cup cream, Salt, Black and Red Pepper, and stir till smooth. Add 1 teaspoon chopped Parsley, 1 cup Bread Crumbs, and 2 beaten Eggs. Thoroughly mix, and add 1 pound Crabmeat. Stuff shells, mounding high; do not mash, or compact the mixture. Sprinkle with Bread Crumbs, run in a hot oven, and bake to a nice brown. In sprinkling Bread Crumbs on Deviled Crabs, do so lightly, as nothing is worse than the average restaurant's practice of armor-plating them.

★ CRAB IMPERIAL

1 pound "Flake," or "Lump" Crabmeat, 1 cup Cream, 1 cup finely chopped Red or Green Pepper, preferably both (for color), 1 cup Bread Crumbs, 1 tablespoon Worcester Sauce, ½ teaspoon dry Mustard, ½ teaspoon Celery Seed, 1 teaspoon Vinegar, Salt and Red Pepper, 1 tablespoon Butter.

Melt Butter, add Cream, Salt, Pepper, Mustard, Worcester, Celery Seed, and Vinegar. When thoroughly mixed and heated, add Red and Green Peppers, Bread Crumbs; mix well, take from fire, and mix in, very gently, the Crabmeat. Stuff shells, mounding highly; remember not to break the lumps of Crabmeat. Sprinkle lightly with Bread Crumbs, and run in hot oven to bake to a nice brown. (Addition of a little Mayonnaise pleases some tastes.)

★ CRAB RAVIGOTE A LA CLEMENTS

Mix chopped Red and Green Peppers with Lump Crabmeat, and Mayonnaise—to make a slightly thick mixture. Stuff shell, mounding high; and brush with Mayonnaise to hold a garnish of finely chopped hard boiled Egg. Cross the top with strips of Red and Green Pepper, put a sliced stuffed Olive in the middle; and set the crab in a nest of shredded lettuce. This is a party dish, and lends itself to very attractive decorations.

★ CRAB CROQUETTES

1 pound Crabmeat, 2 yolks of Eggs, ½ cup Bread Crumbs, 2 yolks of hard boiled Eggs, 2 tablespoons Butter, 1 teaspoon Anchovy Sauce, 1 teaspoon Lemon Juice, little Lemon Peel, Mace, Salt, Black and Red Pepper.

Melt the Butter, and rub in yolks of hard boiled Eggs, add Lemon Juice, Anchovy Sauce, a pinch of grated Lemon Peel, Salt, Black and Red Pepper, Mace, and Crabmeat. Mix thoroughly, then add yolks of raw Eggs and Bread Crumbs. Mould into croquettes, sprinkle with Bread Crumbs, and fry in deep boiling fat.

★ CRAB OLIO

(See recipe for Creamed Crab, p. 33.)

★ CRAB RISSOLES

Mince 1 pound Crabmeat, season with Salt, Black and Red Pepper, Mace and Nutmeg. Add ½ cup Bread Crumbs, and enough Butter to make a stiff mixture. Roll into small balls, dip into Egg yolk, dredge with Flour, and fry in deep boiling fat to a nice brown.

These are to garnish fish dishes; or the mixture may be put into Scallop shells, and baked.

★ CRAB CANTERBURY

1 pound Crabmeat, (preferably part Clawmeat), 2 cups Cream, 1 tablespoon Butter, 1 white of Egg, Salt, Black and Red Pepper, Nutmeg.

Mince Crabmeat, season with Butter, Salt, Black and Red Pepper and Nutmeg, and mix in white of Egg. Let it chill in the refrigerator, then add Cream, and mix until smooth and light. Put into one or more moulds, run in a slow oven to thoroughly heat, without browning. Then, turn out upon a plate, and serve with a Cream Sauce, flavored with Sherry. This is a party dish, so it should be gaily decorated with Parsley, sliced hard boiled Eggs and sliced Olives, and sprinkled with Paprica Pepper.

★ BUTTERED CRAB

Put 1 pound of Crabmeat in a saucepan, with ½ pound Butter, a little Consomme, Salt, Red and Black Pepper, and Nutmeg. Let it simmer 10 minutes; then add Lemon Juice, Vinegar or Sherry, before serving on toast.

★ CREAMED CRAB

Melt 1 tablespoon Butter, stir in 1 tablespoon Flour; when smooth, add 1 cup Milk or Cream, Salt, Black and Red Pepper. Add 1 pound Crabmeat; and, when heated and mixed, add 1 teaspoon chopped Parsley. This may be served on toast, with Sherry; or used to stuff Peppers, or Eggplant. In the latter case, proceed as you would for Stuffed Eggplant, but mix the Creamed Crab into the stuffing. Such a dish is sometimes called *Crab Olio*.

★ CRAB AND MUSHROOMS

1 pound Crabmeat, 1 cup Mushrooms, ½ cup Cream, 2 whites of Egg, 1 teaspoon chopped Parsley, 1 teaspoon Capers, juice ½ a Lemon, 2 tablespoons Butter, 1 tablespoon Flour, Salt and Pepper.

Cook Mushrooms in the Butter, and chop fine. Add to liquor, Flour and Cream, and stir till smooth. Then add, Mushrooms, Crabmeat, Parsley, Capers, Salt, Black and Red Pepper. Mix thoroughly, put in casserole, or in shells, sprinkle with Bread Crumbs, and bake in a moderate oven, about 20 minutes, to a nice brown. Serve with a Sherry Sauce.

★ CRAB CAKES

1 pound Crabmeat, 2 Eggs, 1 finely chopped Onion, (if you like it), 1 cup Bread Crumbs, ¼ teaspoon dry Mustard, or ½ teaspoon prepared Mustard, ½ teaspoon chopped Parsley, 1 tablespoon Mayonnaise, Salt and Red Pepper, dash of Worcester Sauce.

Slightly beat the Eggs, and mix all of the ingredients together. Then form into flat cakes, about an inch thick; and fry in deep boiling fat to a golden brown.

★ CRAB NEWBURG

(See Oyster Newburg, p. 19.)

★ CRAB A LA TALBOT

1 pound Crabmeat, 2 cups Corn, 2 chopped Peppers, 1 chopped small Onion, 1 yolk of Egg, 2 tablespoons Butter, Salt and Pepper.

Brown the Onion in the Butter, add Milk, Corn and Peppers. When Corn is cooked, add Crabmeat, Salt and Red Pepper. Heat and mix thoroughly, add beaten yolk of Egg, and stir until thick. Serve on toast. Garnish with Parsley.

★ CRAB RAMEKINS

1 pound Crabmeat, 1 teaspoon chopped Onion, 1 teaspoon chopped Parsley, 1 teaspoon chopped Celery tops, 1½ cups skimmed Milk, 2 tablespoons Butter, 2 tablespoons Flour, Salt and Pepper.

Brown Onion in Butter, add Flour, and stir until smooth. Add Milk, and when well heated, add other ingredients. Line Ramekins with pastry, fill, cover and pierce crust; and bake about 30 minutes in a moderate oven. Or, you can simply use a top crust, and bake only about 15 minutes.

★ CRAB GLOUCESTER

1 pound Crabmeat, about 4 Potatoes, 2 Egg Yolks, 1 cup Milk, 1 teaspoon chopped Parsley, 6 Anchovies, 2 tablespoons Flour, 2 tablespoons Butter, Salt and Pepper.

Melt Butter, stir in Flour; when smooth add Milk, chopped Anchovies, Salt, Red Pepper, Crabmeat and beaten yolks. Heat and mix thoroughly.

Boil and mash the Potatoes, and beat lightly, with Salt and Parsley, and line a buttered baking dish, or ramekins, with them. Fill with the Crabmeat mixture, cover with a Potato crust, lay over it a piece of oiled paper; and bake in a moderate oven about 20 minutes. Then, turn out upon toast, and pour over them the remains of the Crabmeat mixture.

★ FRICASSEED CRABS

1 pound Crabmeat, 1 pint Tomatoes, 1 pint water, 1 tablespoon Butter, 1 tablespoon Flour, some Onion, Salt and Pepper.

Stew the Tomatoes in the water, add chopped Onion to taste, and Salt and Pepper. Strain through a sieve; add Butter and Flour to thicken, and stew again for about 15 minutes. Then add Crabmeat, heat and mix thoroughly. Serve with steamed Rice.

★ JELLIED CRABMEAT

1 pound Crabmeat, ½ envelope Gelatine, ½ cup cold water, 1½ cups Consomme, 6 Mushrooms, 12 sliced stuffed Olives, 1 tablespoon Capers, 1 tablespoon Lemon Juice.

Soak Gelatine in the cold water, then dissolve in hot Consomme, and let cool. Then, add the other ingredients, pour into mould, and chill in refrigerator. Garnish with Egg, Lemon, Parsley and Lettuce.

★ CRAB COCKTAIL

2 cups "Flake" or "Lump" Crabmeat, 2 tablespoons Horseradish, 3 tablespoons Tomato Ketchup, 1 tablespoon Lemon Juice, 1 tablespoon Worcester Sauce, 1 or 2 dashes Tabasco Sauce, Salt.

Mix the seasonings together, and put in refrigerator to chill. Just before serving, add the Crabmeat—gently, so as not to break it up. Serve in a cocktail glass, and garnish with an Olive.

CRAWFISH

Probably the least known of the Chesapeake's denizens is that dainty little morsel the Crawfish, which is found in great abundance in the Potomac and Susquehanna Rivers. It is a miniature Lobster, about 5 inches long, and almost as black as the ace of spades. Many years ago, it was in such tremendous demand in the "foreign" markets of New York and New Orleans, that Montreal and Milwaukee were called upon to supply the over-demand; and, at the latter place, the business justified its propagation.

The Crawfish is a delicious viand, and is in season from the breaking up of the ice in the spring to the next winter's freeze. Its only drawback is its tough shell, which must be broken with a rolling-pin or hammer to reach the meat in the tail which is, in size, about as big as that of a Shrimp. Its claw meat, too, is piquant, but it is only about as big as a peanut. Crawfish must be steamed, like Crab, only with a great deal of salt, as it comes from fresher waters. It can be eaten "just-so," or it can be prepared according to Crab, Shrimp and Lobster recipes.

LOBSTER

★ **LOBSTER**

It was not for want of the attempt by the Maryland Fish Commissioners, in the 1870's, that the Chesapeake Bay did not prove congenial to the Lobsters imported hither, with a hope of establishing the crustacean in the Bay. But the experiment proved a failure; and the closest Lobsters we have had are those that "took" in the rocks of the Delaware Bay breakwater, now depleted by too-ardent fishermen. Nevertheless, the Bay's inhabitants are great consumers of the northern delicacy.

★ TO BOIL AND OPEN A LOBSTER

Put Lobster head-down in a kettle of warm, not boiling, water, with a tablespoon of Salt; cover, and put over a quick fire. A medium Lobster should boil ½ hour, a large one, ¾ hour. If you cook them too long the meat will be tough, and stick to the shell. When done, cool, separate the shells, twist off the claws and legs; shake out the "Tom Alley," or green liver; also the coral. Draw the body from the shell, remove the stomach, or the "Lady," immediately under the head, then split the body, and pick the meat from the cells. Cut the under-side of the tail, and take the meat out whole. Then split the meat, and take out the vein running its length. This is sometimes red, black or white, but it must be removed carefully. The stomach, vein and the spongy fingers, or "Deadmen" between the body and the shell, are the only parts not edible. Crack the claws, and remove their meat.

★ LOBSTER NEWBURG

(See recipe for Oyster Newburg, p. 19.)

★ LOBSTER FARCI

2 cups boiled Lobster, yolks 3 hardboiled Eggs, 1 tablespoon chopped Parsley, 1 tablespoon Bread Crumbs, ½ pint Milk, 1 level tablespoon Flour, 1 tablespoon Butter, Salt and Red Pepper, Nutmeg.

Cut the Lobster into small pieces. Bring Milk to a boil, add Butter rubbed with Flour, stir until smooth. Take off fire, add Bread Crumbs, Parsley, Lobster, Salt, Red Pepper, Nutmeg, and yolks of Eggs mashed fine. Mix thoroughly, and stuff Lobster tail; sprinkle with Bread Crumbs, and run in quick oven, for 15 minutes, to brown nicely. Garnish with Parsley.

★ LOBSTER CHOPS

2 cups boiled Lobster, 1 cup Cream or Milk, 1 tablespoon chopped Parsley, yolks 2 Eggs, 1 tablespoon Butter, 3 tablespoons Flour, Salt and Red Pepper, Nutmeg.

Add all the seasoning to the chopped Lobster. Bring Cream or Milk to a boil, add Butter rubbed with Flour,—stir till smooth; add beaten yolks, and cook 2 minutes, then add Lobster, mix thoroughly and let cool. Form into chops, roll in beaten Egg, then in Bread Crumbs; and fry to a nice brown in deep boiling fat. Stick the chops with a claw, to resemble a "bone," garnish with Parsley; and serve with a Cream or Tartar Sauce.

★ SCALLOPED LOBSTER

6 pounds live Lobster, ½ pint Milk, 1 tablespoon chopped Parsley, ½ cup Bread Crumbs, 1 tablespoon Butter, 1 tablespoon Flour, Salt and Red Pepper.

Bring Milk to a boil, add Butter rubbed with Flour. Meanwhile, boil and clean the Lobsters. Put a layer of White Sauce in baking dish, then a layer of Lobster, sprinkle with Salt and Red Pepper, and so on, mixing in the Parsley. Let the last layer be of sauce, cover with Bread Crumbs, and put in a quick oven, for 15 minutes, to brown nicely.

★ LOBSTER WITH CECIL SAUCE

Boil the Lobster, and cut meat in pieces about an inch square. Melt 1 tablespoon Butter, add 1 tablespoon Flour, stir till smooth, add 1 gill Cream, and 1 gill Fish Stock (see recipe, p. 53), stir to a boil. Add Lobster, Salt and Red Pepper. Heat and mix thoroughly, and take from fire. Add beaten yolk of an Egg, and 1 tablespoon chopped Parsley, also a little Sherry, if you wish. This may be served in individual dishes, or be used as a filling for patties.

★ DEVILED LOBSTER

(See recipe for Deviled Crab, p. 31.)

SHRIMP

Shrimp is the great southern Crustacean. It comes no closer to the Chesapeake Bay than the Carolinas, but it appears in our markets throughout the entire year, and is thoroughly enjoyed by the gourmets. As a rule only the tails containing the meat are available. They should first be steamed about 20-25 minutes in a little water, (about 1½ inches deep in the kettle), highly seasoned with Salt, Red Pepper, Mustard and Vinegar; if you wish to eat the steamed Shrimp, add Black Pepper and Celery Seed. After removing the shell with a sharp-pointed knife, lift out the little triangular piece on the back of the meat with the vein under it, running the full length of the meat. This must be removed, and the vein scraped clean.

Many of the recipes for Crab and Lobster do equally well for Shrimp, therefore we only add a few particular ones.

★ CREOLE GUMBO

1 Chicken, 1 sliced Onion, 2 dozen or more Oysters, several pieces of Ham, diced, 1 quart Shrimp, 1½ quarts water, 1 teaspoon chopped Parsley, 1 little hot Red Pepper, 1 tablespoon Flour, Salt, Black Pepper, 1 pint cup Okra.

Cut the Chicken into small pieces, and fry in hot lard; then add Onion, Oysters and Ham, and fry until brown; then add Flour, and stir in. Take out Oysters, add water, Pepper, and Okra, and boil one hour. Take out the hot Pepper, and add Parsley, Salt and Black Pepper; (the dish is not supposed to be "hot"). Add Shrimp, and put back Oysters, simmer 15 minutes, pour into a tureen, and add plenty of steamed Rice. This is a delightful meal-unto-itself.

★ SHRIMP NEWBURG

(See recipe for Oyster Newburg, p. 19.)

★ SHRIMP PASTE

Pound steamed Shrimp, add plenty of Butter, until you have a smooth paste; season with Salt, Black and Red Pepper, and

Nutmeg. Then put into moulds, and bake about 20 minutes in a moderate oven, to a nice brown.

★ PICKLED SHRIMP

Boil steamed Shrimp in strongly salted water, allowing ½ cup water to 1 pound Shrimp, for about 15 minutes. Remove Shrimp, drain and put in a crock. Then boil ⅓ water, and ⅔ Vinegar, sufficient to cover the Shrimp by 2 inches; let cool, and pour over Shrimp. Cover crock tightly, and they will keep for some time.

★ FRIED SHRIMP

1 pound Shrimp, ½ cup Milk, 1 beaten Egg, Flour, Nutmeg, Salt and Red Pepper.

Put seasonings in Milk and pour over the Shrimp, stir a few minutes, then pour off. Add Egg to the Milk, and mix. Sprinkle the Shrimp lightly with Flour, dip them into the Milk, then into Bread Crumbs, Cracker Dust, or Cornmeal; fry in hot fat. Serve with Lemon and Parsley.

★ CHICKEN AND SHRIMP GUMBO

1 Chicken, 1 slice Ham, ½ pint Okra, 8 Tomatoes, 1 pound Shrimp, 1 Onion, Salt, Black and Red Pepper, little Thyme.

Boil Chicken in 1½ gallons water, till reduced one-half. Remove Chicken, cut into pieces, and fry, with Onion and Ham. Put all of this back into water, add Tomatoes and chopped Okra, and boil about 2 hours. Then add Shrimp, and simmer 15 minutes. Season with Salt, Black and Red Pepper and Thyme. Serve with steamed Rice.

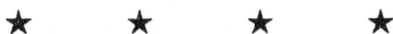

★　　★　　★　　★　　*Fin Fish*

★ TO BOIL FISH

All fish, except Salmon, should be put in cold salted water, with a little Lemon Juice or Vinegar. Then, it should boil very gently, or the outside will break before the inside is done. It must be taken from the water the instant it is done, or it will become insipid, watery and colorless. Experience alone can teach you when to take it out. A large fish should boil about 8 minutes to the pound, and a small one about 5 minutes to the pound. Use only enough water to cover the fish. Fresh water fish, with no decided flavor, may be boiled with Onions, Carrots, Parsley, Cloves, Pepper, Salt, Vinegar or Wine—to taste. If you will first wrap the fish in a cloth, when it is done you may lift it with that and possibly save breaking it.

★ TO FRY FISH

Preferably, fish should be fried in boiling fat sufficiently deep to cover the fish. Bacon drippings are ideal. Be sure the fat is hot enough, otherwise the fish will absorb some of the fat, and make a greasy dish.

Fish to be fried should be dredged with flour, brushed with beaten egg, and then rolled in cracker dust or bread crumbs. Brown first on one side, and then the other. When done, drain, or lay upon brown paper, so that the fish may be quite dry.

★ TO BROIL FISH

Fish prepared in this manner is not only delicious, but free of grease from frying, or panning, that puts the fat upon oneself. If a fish is small, it requires a hot fire; if it be large, a moderate one will suffice, otherwise the outside will be burned before the inside is cooked. A dry fish, like Spanish Mackerel, should be rubbed with a little Olive oil to prevent it from drying over, or under, the fire. When the fish is done,

41

sprinkle with salt and pepper, a few drops of lemon, chopped parsley, and melted butter; then put it into the oven for a moment, to let the seasonings soak into it.

★ TO BAKE FISH

Baked fish are often stuffed and sewn, or wrapped with cord, to retain the stuffing. Put in the baking pan, with a little hot water. Cover with several strips of bacon under the cords, if it is wrapped, sprinkle with Pepper, Salt and Bread Crumbs; and bake to a nice brown. Baste frequently, otherwise the fish will be quite dry, and not very palatable. A simple Drawn Butter Sauce, with Lemon Juice and Pepper is very acceptable, if time does not permit something more elaborate.

★ TO PLANK FISH

The plank should be well-seasoned Oak or Hickory, 2-3 inches thick, 1½ feet wide, and 2 feet long. Clean, split, dry a Shad, Rock, Bluefish, etc., and dredge with Salt and Pepper. Put plank in front of fire, get it very hot, then tack the fish, skin side to it, large end down. As the fish cooks before the fire, up-end the plank every few minutes. Pierce with a fork, to see if the meat is flaky and cooked; then spread with melted Butter, and serve direct from the plank.

★ TO GARNISH FISH DISHES

(See recipe for Crab Rissoles, p. 32.)

★ TO FILLET FISH

(See Foreword, p. 5.)

★ BAKED BLUEFISH, No. 1

Stuff with Bread Crumbs, Salt, Pepper and a hint of Sage, or Thyme, and sew it up. Sprinkle with Flour, and cover with several slices of Bacon. Put a little water in the pan, with a sprig of Parsley, slice of Onion, cut up Carrot, Salt and Pepper. Bake one hour in a hot oven. Baste first with melted Butter, and then with the pan liquor.

★ BAKED BLUEFISH, No. 2

Split and lay skin down in the pan, and bake in a hot oven about 30 minutes. Put in the pan 2 tablespoons Butter, juice ½ Lemon, a little Onion, Salt, Pepper, and just enough water to allow you to spoon-up the mixture. Baste frequently, and serve with the pan liquor as a gravy.

★ BLUEFISH A L'ITALIENNE

Do not stuff the fish, but lay it in the pan. Add 3 tablespoons white Wine, 3 tablespoons Mushroom Catsup, ½ chopped Onion, 1 dozen chopped Mushrooms, 1 tablespoon Butter, and a little water. Bake 45 minutes in a hot oven; baste frequently. Serve with the pan liquor. Garnish with Parsley.

★ STEWED CARP

Clean, wash and dry with a clean cloth; dredge with Flour, and fry in boiling fat, until brown. Then put in a pan with 1 cup water, 1 cup Red Wine, 1 tablespoon Lemon Juice, 1 tablespoon Mushroom Catsup, an Onion stuck with Cloves, little Horseradish, Salt, Black and Red Pepper. Cover, and simmer until gravy covers the fish. Then, put the Carp on a hot dish, thicken liquor with Butter and Flour, strain and pour over dish. Garnish with pickled Mushrooms, and Horseradish.

★ CATFISH SOUP

After cleaning and skinning 3-4 Catfish, (and taking off the heads and tails), cut each into 3 pieces. Put into pot with 1 pound chopped Bacon, 1 chopped Onion, 3 tablespoons chopped

Parsley, Salt and Pepper, cover with water and stew until tender. Melt 1 tablespoon Butter, stir in 2 tablespoons Flour, add 1 cup of Milk; when heated, add beaten yolks of 4 Eggs, mix thoroughly and add to soup. Stir until it thickens, and serve.

★ CROAKER, HARDHEAD, or KING BILLY

Named "Croaker," because of its audible "croak," both in and out of the water,—named "Hardhead" by Captain Julius Digges of Virginia, because when he spread them upon his fields for fertilizer their heads would not rot,—called "King Billy" in Virginia, after William Claiborne, who croaked ever-after when his domain of Kent Island was grabbed by Lord Baltimore. To some, it is a very coarse fish; but if it is killed the instant it is landed, its flavor is greatly improved. When boiled and picked, the Croaker's firm, flaky meat has proved a blessing to many desperate hostesses, by way of "padding" Crab dishes for unexpected guests.

★ STEWED CROAKER

Clean the fish, remove the head and tail, cover well with Salt and let stand for an hour or two. Then, put it in the pot, add ½ an Onion, Salt and Pepper, and boil until tender. Remove, and put on a hot plate. Rub 2 tablespoons Flour into 1 tablespoon Butter, add teaspoon chopped Parsley, and 1 cupful of the pot liquor. Stir smooth, add juice ½ a Lemon, and pour into the pot. Stir until heated, then pour over the fish.

★ BAKED CROAKER

Clean and boil the fish in salted water, until tender; then remove skin, bones, head and tail. Put a layer of fish in the baking dish, sprinkle with Salt and Pepper, then a layer of Bread Crumbs, and so on, until dish is filled. Boil 1 pint Milk with an Onion, until Milk is flavored, then strain and pour into dish; bake in moderate oven 40 minutes, until a nice brown.

★ FLOUNDER (FILLETED)

Clean, and cut into fillets. Take head, tail, skin, bones and trimmings, add Parsley, Onion, Celery tops, 6 Peppercorns, Allspice. Cover with water, and simmer one-half away. Strain, and let cool; and you have Fish Stock. Put fillets in covered pan, add Salt, Pepper, Lemon Juice, 2 tablespoons White Wine, and let simmer for 15-20 minutes, until tender. Serve with this sauce;—2 tablespoons Butter, 2 tablespoons Flour, 1 cup Fish Stock, yolks 2 Eggs, 2 tablespoons Cream, 1 teaspoon chopped Parsley, 2 dozen Mushrooms, 2 tablespoons White Wine, Salt, Black and Red Pepper. Melt the Butter, stir in the Flour and Fish Stock until it thickens, add beaten yolks, Cream and seasonings, then chopped cooked Mushrooms, Parsley and Wine. Heat thoroughly, and pour over dish. Garnish with sliced Lemon.

Fillets of any fish can also be simply bread-crumbed and fried; or flaked and baked.

★ HERRING

The ancient saying that "Amsterdam is built upon Herring bones" is equally good of Baltimore, Norfolk and Havre de Grace. In the beginning, Chesapeake Bay colonists planted but one crop—tobacco; that, with walnut timber, formed their principal exports. For over a century, they were beggared by this single-cropping which persisted in spite of revolutionary attempts to broaden their agriculture. Then in the middle of the 1700's, the Carrolls, of Maryland, opened their vast western lands, established the millers Ellicott outside of Baltimore, and practically compelled their tenants to raise grain instead of tobacco. This was followed by a similar trend on the Eastern Shore, which led to Maryland's trade with the West Indies. She exported wheat, corn, salt pork and salt fish, to feed the Islands' slaves, and imported their sugar, rum, coffee and spices, thus stimulating the Baltimore "Clipper Ship" era.

Another demand came from the Pennsylvania Dutch farmers, who migrated each spring to the Chesapeake Bay to get their winter's supply of salt Herring and Shad. In the 1880's Baltimore was still one of the nation's foremost salt centers, because of her importations of that essential to the Bay's salt fish industry.

★ FRESH HERRING

Clean the fish, but do not scale it. Split down the backbone, salt well, and let stand 24 hours. Then, Pepper heavily, fold together, put in the pan with a little water, and cover with sliced Bacon. Put in moderate oven, and bake until brown; then turn over, and brown other side. Serve by opening fish, and laying the Bacon on the inside.

★ FRESH HERRING ROE

Boil the Roe in salted water, 2-3 minutes, and drain. Then put in a pan, with Butter and Lemon juice, run in a moderate oven, and bake for about 15 minutes. If you wish, you can bake it with Lemon Juice and Bacon. In either case, baste frequently.

★ HERRING ROE CROQUETTES

(See recipe for Shad Roe Croquettes, p. 49.)

★ POTTED HERRING

Scale, clean, cut off heads and tails, wash well and wipe dry. Rub with a mixture of Salt, Black and Red Pepper, and any other spice you wish. Then put the Herring in layers in a crock, or porcelain kettle, cover with Vinegar, and simmer 3-4 hours, replacing any Vinegar that is lost. Let cool, and keep a few days before eating with an Oil dressing.

★ SMOKED HERRING

It is an old Baltimore tradition that you should eat a Smoked Herring for New Year's breakfast, if you wish good luck for the rest of the year. We admit the smell when cooking is powerful, and we further admit to wishing it strong enough to awaken us. But we insist that few dishes can equal it as a delicacy.

Soak the Herring overnight; drain in the morning, and slit along the belly; be careful not to break the roe. Put in a pan with a little water, and run in a moderate oven, for about 15-20 minutes, until it curls, and is cooked. Baste several times. Serve with Toast, or Hot Cakes.

★ SPANISH MACKEREL

May be either stuffed and baked, or split and broiled. Or—clean, remove head and tail, and split down the backbone. Rub with a little Butter or Olive Oil, sprinkle with Salt and Pepper, pour over it a scant cup of Milk, and bake in a hot oven for 20 minutes. Baste frequently.

★ SALT MACKEREL

Soak overnight in cold water. In the morning, drain, and broil about 5 minutes, on each side. Or, put in a pan with a tablespoon of Butter, run in a hot oven, and let simmer 15-20 minutes, covered. Sprinkle with Black Pepper, Lemon juice, and serve with Melted Butter.

★ NORFOLK SPOT, YELLOW AND WHITE PERCH

It is doubtful if there are more delicious pan-fish than these three inhabitants of the Chesapeake Bay. They are usually served fried, either with or without their heads and tails taken off. At the Carroll's Island Ducking Club, they were skinned and boned, lightly sprinkled with Salt and Pepper, and sauted in Butter. When you fry them, do not overdo dipping them in Bread Crumbs or Cornmeal; cook them in deep hot fat—so that they will not be greasy.

★ ROCK (Striped Bass)

One of the Chesapeake Bay's celebrated fish, (empirically called the Stripe-ed Bass) ; named, according to Captain John Smith, "from his hew and haunting amongst the rocks."

While many of its tribe pass in and out of the Bay, the Rock is indigenous to the Chesapeake, where it ranges from the small pan-fish which are sweetest, to immense 60 pounders. Its flesh is a beautiful white, very firm, yet not dry. The Rock can be cooked in many ways, but the favorite manner of boiling it produces a noble dish. It is customary to leave the head and tail on, and wrap the Rock in a cloth, so as to lift it from the boiling water without breaking. Add to the water a heaping tablespoon of Salt, a little Vinegar, and let simmer gently about 10 minutes to the pound. Turn out upon a platter, serve with a White Sauce, Hollandaise, Caper, Shrimp, Oyster or Crab Sauce. Garnish with thinly sliced Lemon, sliced hard boiled Egg and Parsley. Rock is a dish that well deserves attractive decoration.

★ SOUSED ROCK

Boil a fair size Rock until the meat can be taken from the bones; let cool, cut into pieces, and put in a crock. Boil Vinegar, sufficient to cover the fish, with Cloves, Allspice, Mace, Peppercorns and Salt. When cold, pour into crock, cover tightly, and keep in a cool place. The Rock should not be eaten for a day or so.

★ SHAD

Captain Basil Hall, who came hither in the late 1820's, wrote of the "glorious breakfast" he enjoyed upon his landing;—"We had asked merely for some fresh Shad, a fish reputed to be excellent, as indeed, it proved. The Shad is a native of American waters, I believe, exclusively, and if so, it is almost worthy of a voyage across the Atlantic to make its acquaintance." An appreciation of the Shad has always existed on the Chesapeake Bay, where that fish reaches its perfection of flavor. In this modern day, when we neglect, (as much as we can), bothersome things, the Shad is overlooked because of its bones. The trick of removing those irritations has been discovered; but, as the method would be complicated to explain, it may be easily learned from one who knows how, and the procedure takes only about ten minutes. However, about one-half of the fish's weight is lost, and the remainder can only be panned or broiled. An old time way of removing the bones was to dissolve them by baking the Shad, in a covered pan, frequently basting with very little water, for 6½ hours.

★ STUFFED SHAD

Wash and wipe clean, but do not soak. Make a stuffing of 1 cup Bread Crumbs, 1 tablespoon chopped Parsley, 1 table-

spoon Butter, ½ teaspoon Salt, ½ teaspoon Pepper, pinch of
Sage. Stuff the fish, and sew it up. With a sharp knife,
make scores across one side, one inch apart; and lay a strip
of Bacon in each. Grease the baking pan, lay Bacon on the
bottom, put the fish atop of it, dredge with Flour, Salt and
Pepper, and add a little boiling water. Bake in a moderate
oven, 15 minutes to the pound, basting frequently; add water
if necessary. Then, slide the fish upon a platter, and garnish
with Parsley, sliced Lemon and Potato balls. The roe also
may be cooked in the pan, put in when the fish is half-done,
and turned over several times.

★ SHAD ROE

May be sauted in Butter, or with Bacon. In either case,
cook it slowly, with a little Salt and Pepper, basting with
Lemon juice. Turn over frequently, and allow about 15-20
minutes to cook thoroughly, as it is insipid when half-cooked.
Serve garnished with Parsley, and quartered Lemon.

★ SHAD, OR HERRING ROE CROQUETTES

1 pair Shad Roes, or 6 pairs fresh Herring Roes, yolks 2
Eggs, 1 cup Cream, 1 teaspoon, or more, Lemon juice, 1 table-
spoon chopped Parsley, 1 tablespoon Butter, 2 tablespoons
Flour, Salt and Pepper, Nutmeg.

Simmer in a little salted water for about 15 minutes. Then
drain, skin and mash, or rather, separate the eggs. Melt Butter, stir in Flour, add Cream, and boil until very thick, then
add beaten yolks of Eggs, Salt and Pepper, Lemon juice,

Parsley and Nutmeg. As it cools, add the mashed Roes; and when cold, form into croquettes, dip into beaten Egg, then into Bread Crumbs, and fry in deep boiling fat. Serve with Hollandaise Sauce.

★ BROILED SALT SHAD

Soak overnight in cold water; then drain for an hour. Grease the gridiron, and broil—inside towards the fire, first.

★ BOILED SALT SHAD, HERRING OR MACKEREL

Wash the pickle off, put in a frying pan, cover with water, and boil 15-25 minutes, according to the size of the fish. Drain, pour a Drawn Butter Sauce, with Lemon, over the fish, and serve.

★ SMELTS

Another fish that the Bay's first Fish Commissioners unsuccessfully attempted to establish in the Chesapeake.

Smelts should be lightly dipped into Beaten Egg, then into Bread Crumbs, and fried, preferably in drippings. Serve with Tartar Sauce.

CHOWDERS, MUDDLES, ETC.

★ BOUILLABAISSE

(The French Idea of a Chowder)

2 pounds mixed fish, (not of the oily varieties, like Shad or Mackerel), ¼ pound Crabmeat, 1 Onion, 1 teaspoon or more chopped Parsley, 2 chopped Tomatoes, 4 tablespoons Olive Oil, 1 clove, Salt, Black and Red Pepper, ⅛ teaspoon Saffron, 1 wineglass White Wine.

Boil fish heads and save the liquor. Boil fish livers, drain and chop. Skin and bone the fish, and chop the meat. Slice Onion, and fry in Olive Oil, then add fish, and fry. Then add Tomatoes, liquor from fish heads, Parsley, seasonings; let come to a boil, and add Crabmeat. Boil 10 minutes, add

Saffron, and take off the instant the fish is tender. Some like to add a little Garlic. Serve over Toast cut into cubes.

★ FISH CHOWDER

Everybody seems to have his own idea as to contriving a Chowder; therefore, the following is more of a suggestion than a recipe.

3 pounds Fish, 1 pint Milk, 3 Potatoes, 2 cups Tomatoes, 1 Onion, ¼ pound sliced Bacon or Ham, 1 quart water, 1 tablespoon Thyme, 1 teaspoon Sweet Marjoram, Salt, Black and Red Pepper, Sea Biscuits.

Cut the Fish, Potatoes, Onion and Bacon into ½ inch pieces. Fry Onion and Bacon to a nice brown. Put into baking dish a layer of Potatoes, layer of Fish, layer of Onion and Bacon, layer of Tomatoes, and so on; season each layer; add water, cover and simmer 20 minutes without stirring. Boil Milk 3 minutes, with broken Biscuits (about 3 are enough); add to Chowder, stir to a boil, taste and re-season, if necessary, and serve.

★ FISH A LA QUEEN ANNE

1 pound picked, left-over boiled fish, 3-4 chopped cooked Mushrooms, 1 tablespoon chopped Parsley, 1 cup Milk or Cream, yolk of 1 Egg, 1 tablespoon Butter, 1 tablespoon Flour, Salt and Pepper, Sherry.

Melt Butter, stir in Flour, add Milk, and bring to a boil, stir till smooth. Then add fish, Mushrooms, Salt and Pepper. When thoroughly heated, add beaten yolk of Egg and Parsley; mix thoroughly, and add 1 tablespoon, or more, Sherry, as you take it from the fire. Serve in shells, or in ramekins.

★ A MUDDLE

This our great-grandparents served at their beach picnics.

Clean and cut a Shad, Rock or Pike into pieces, and put, alternately with slices of Salt Pork (Fat-back) into a Dutch oven, (a deep cast iron skillet); adding Salt, Black and Red Pepper, and just enough water "as may leave it doubtful if the Muddle is a stew or a soup." When it is half-done, plunge into the boiling mass slices of Corn Bread, in proportion of ¼ of the Muddle. "Wash down with Applejack."

★ LEFT-OVER FISH

2 cups Fish, Butter, Parsley, ½ sliced Onion, ½ cup Bread Crumbs, 1 cup White Sauce, Salt, Black and Red Pepper.

Pick the Fish, put a layer in a buttered dish, then a layer of White Sauce, with Onion and chopped Parsley, Salt and Pepper, and so on. Cover with Bread Crumbs, and bake to a nice brown. A little Lemon Juice may be added to flavor.

★ FISH BALLS

Mix and press through a colander, 1 cup left-over Fish, and 1 cup cold boiled Potatoes. Mix thoroughly, season with Salt and Pepper, roll into balls, dip in beaten Egg, then into Bread Crumbs, and fry in deep boiling fat to a nice brown.

★ JELLIED FISH

2 pounds any steak Fish, 6 stuffed Olives, 1 hard boiled Egg, 2 cups strained Tomatoes, 1 teaspoon Onion juice, 1 tablespoon Worcester Sauce, ½ thin sliced Lemon, 1 package Gelatine, Salt and Pepper.

Boil Fish in 3 cups water, with 1 whole Mace and 1 Bay leaf, for 10 minutes; remove Fish, and boil stock down to 2 cups. Strain, and add Tomatoes, Onion and Seasonings. Dissolve Gelatine, and add to boiling stock. Pick the Fish from bones and skin, and put in a cold mould; with Egg, Olives and Lemon, pour in stock; put in refrigerator to stiffen. Turn out on a large plate, that you may have plenty of room to garnish it attractively with Lettuce, Parsley, Lemon, Egg, Olives, etc. Serve with Tartar Sauce or Mayonnaise.

★ FISH A LA CREME, IN RAMEKINS

2 cups left-over Fish, (either fried or boiled), 1 cup Milk, 2 yolks of Egg, Onion Juice, Salt, Black and Red Pepper, Paprika, 2 tablespoons Butter, 1 tablespoon Flour.

Melt Butter, add Flour and stir till smooth, add Milk and Egg yolks beaten together; then stir till thick and smooth.

Add picked Fish, and seasonings, thoroughly mix and heat. Fill the ramekins, cover with Bread Crumbs, and bits of Butter, and bake to a nice brown. Garnish with Parsley, dust with Paprica.

★ FISH CROQUETTES

Chop left-over Fish very fine, add ⅓ as many mashed Potatoes, and mix to a thick paste with Melted Butter; add White Sauce, chopped Parsley, Salt and Pepper, and Anchovy Sauce. Form into croquettes, dip into beaten Egg, then into Bread Crumbs, and fry in deep boiling fat. Serve with sliced Lemon and a Wine Sauce.

★ FISH STOCK

5 pounds Shad, Rock, Croaker, Blue or Trout, scaled, cleaned and cut into pieces. 1 Onion, 1 stalk Celery, 2 sprigs Parsley, 2 Bay Leaves, 4 whole Cloves, Pepper, 3 quarts water.

Put all into a kettle, bring to a boil, then skim, and let simmer for 2 hours. Strain, and add 1 tablespoon Salt. This can be kept as stock, or served as a clear soup with Croutons.

★ STEWED EELS

2 Eels, ½ cup Consomme, ½ small Onion, 1 dessertspoon Butter, 1 dessertspoon Flour, Salt and Pepper, Parsley.

Skin and clean the Eels, cut into pieces 2 inches long; simmer in water for 10 minutes, with tablespoon Vinegar; then drain. Rub Butter and Flour, add to liquor, with Onion, Salt and Pepper, and a little Parsley. Stir to a boil, add Eels, and stew for 30 minutes, until tender. Put on a hot dish, and pour strained liquor over them.

★ FRIED EELS

Skin, clean and cut into pieces, and parboil in water, with 1 tablespoon Vinegar; then drain and dry. Mix Salt and Pepper, with a little boiling water, to yolk of 1 Egg; dip the Eels into it, then into Bread Crumbs or Corn Meal, and fry in deep hot fat. Serve with Tartar Sauce.

★ PITCHCOCKED EELS

Skin, clean, cut into pieces, wash, and dry with a cloth. Roll in a mixture of Salt, Pepper, and a little Sage. Then skewer, broil to a nice brown, and serve with melted Butter; garnish with fried Parsley.

★ FRIED FROGS LEGS

Put in Salted boiling water with a little Lemon juice, boil for 3 minutes. Wipe clean; then dip first in Cracker Crumbs, then in mixture of 2 beaten Eggs, Milk and Salt and Pepper, then again in Cracker Crumbs. When breaded, clean off bone end with cloth, put in wire basket and dip in boiling lard to fry. Serve immediately—a delicious dish.

★

INDEX